Houses in Cities

TINY

RIZZOLI
NEW YORK

New York Paris London Milan

Mimi Zeiger

First published in the United States of America in 2016 by
RIZZOLI INTERNATIONAL PUBLICATIONS, INC.
300 Park Avenue South
New York, NY 10010
www.rizzoliusa.com

ISBN-13: 978-0-8478-4822-5
Library of Congress Control Numbe: 2015957386

Distributed to the U.S. trade by Random House, New York

Designed by over,under

Printed and bound in China

2016 2017 2018 2019 2020 / 10 9 8 7 6 5 4 3 2 1

Introduction Mimi Zieger

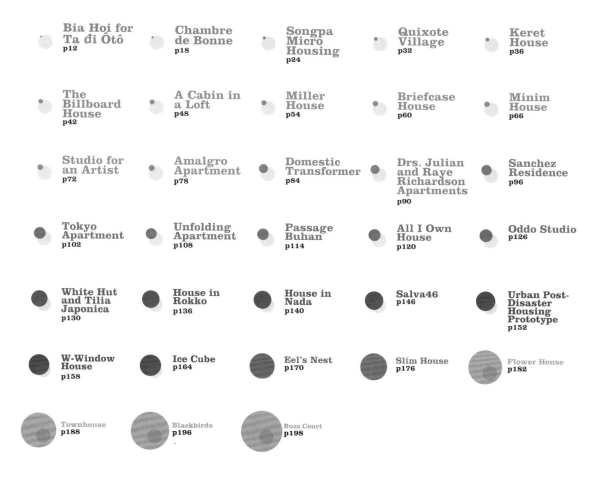

Architects

One June evening not so long ago I was sitting on the roof of a prewar apartment building in Brooklyn. A friend owned a one-bedroom apartment a couple of floors below, and we had retreated to the rooftop with some wine and cheese to escape the stuffy rooms. At five stories up, we were above the street and the trees. The vantage point gave us a sweeping view of the Brooklyn waterfront (awaiting a controversial housing development), of the Hudson River and Lady Liberty, and of Lower Manhattan. As the sun dropped toward the horizon, its rays glinted off the facets of the recently completed One World Trade Center and the Art Deco icon, the Chrysler building. The Big Apple looked incredible—like Oz, not Gotham.

An architecture professor I know joined us on the roof and gazed out over the view. "There are generations of people moving to urban areas with no memory of the city as a dark and scary place," he reflected. The statement, tossed off over a glass of rosé, struck me as profound, even if a tad overstated. If urbanization and industrialization marked the nineteenth and early twentieth century, the second half of the twentieth century in the United States saw the ramifications of city life lead to the systematic decentralization of metropolitan areas. As cultural change and the social unrest of the 1960s was acted out on the streets, cities were increasingly characterized in charged terms such as "cramped," "dirty," or "violent." Urban renewal aimed to wipe out slums and crime, but the efforts often involved an erasure of the urban fabric. The housing projects that then sprung up in so-called blighted neighborhoods often only exacerbated the social problems they were designed to fix. As such, for those with income and mobility the suburbs with sprawling lawns and ballooning home sizes offered a welcoming alternative to inner-city ills. For decades, the ever-growing suburbs represented a lifestyle pinnacle.

This trend, however, is reversing. According to 2013 U.S. Census Bureau data, population in urban areas has steadily increased since 2010, with a total 269.9 million people living in metropolitan areas. The demographic turnaround can be attributed in part to a change in values that follow the redevelopment of inner core areas and a recognition of the benefits of city life: walkable and bike-able neighborhoods, public transit, and cultural institutions. Capital investment in urban amenities and public-private partnerships have led to design innovations that improve the quality of urban life. Among the best-known examples is the High Line, an approximately 1.5-mile-long park built on top of a disused rail spur on Manhattan's West Side. The grassroots effort to preserve and retrofit this abandoned piece of infrastructure sparked renewed private investment in the area and was the impetus for the construction of new housing, hotels, restaurants, and most spectacularly a new building for the Whitney Museum.

Cities across the globe, and especially in the U.S., have shaken off old fears and clichés. Young professionals and baby boomers alike now call a metropolis home and it is suburbia that bears the cast of suspicion. The dark side of unsustainable, unchecked suburban development was made visible with the bust of the housing bubble in the late 2000s. Images of abandoned, half-constructed subdivisions and foreclosed homes boarded up with plywood filled the news. These domestic wastelands underscored the folly of growth, of too many rooms filled with too much stuff.

The tiny house movement developed under these conditions as a critique of a supersized American Dream. Its advocates bear an impetus to reduce impact and position themselves against an abundant consumerism, which gives you big spaces and then makes you want to fill them. The depths of the economic downturn are behind us and a widespread embrace of small spaces has emerged—a Walden to call our own. We've become familiar with the hallmarks of DIY tiny houses: the cabin-like homes built on top of trailers, loft beds, efficient storage, and off-grid amenities. In the media, tiny house living is something of a phenomenon, an obsession to some, an extreme sport to others. Websites routinely gush over well-appointed small spaces, leveraging the Japanese concept of *kawaii*. The term means more than cute; it is the quality of cuteness and the satisfaction of understanding the whole space at once. A sure sign that tiny houses hit the mainstream: the TV show *Portlandia* created a spot-on spoof, with comedian Fred Armisen squeezed into his locker-sized "home-office," a clever space-saving solution gone awry. But what does it mean when the principles of compact design are applied to city living?

To understand how the tiny house movement dovetails with urban life, we first have to understand the pressures of the densifying metropolis. The beautiful view of the Manhattan skyline only hints at the extreme property market in the city, which is driving real estate prices sky-high and compounding social inequity between those who can afford the million-dollar condos in super-skinny luxury towers and those who are desperately in need of affordable housing. "What drives prices skyward is a collision between rampant demand and limited supply in the great metropolises like London, Mumbai and New York," notes *The Economist* in an April 2015 issue. "In the past ten years real prices in Hong Kong have risen by 150%. Residential property in Mayfair, in central London, can go for as much as £55,000 ($82,000) per square meter. A square mile of Manhattan residential property costs $16.5 billion."

Tiny houses and microunits can address this scarcity to a degree. With housing in demand within areas of limited land availability, homes with smaller square-footage fit into spaces that would have previously gone unbuilt, while microunit apartment buildings prioritize good design and shared amenities. Both maximize the architectural potential of any given lot. Moreover, by creating housing in cities, rather than in the suburbs, tiny urban strategies can help counter displacement and strengthen neighborhoods, which is good for the health of the city. The same *Economist* article reported that when property values balloon, only a few reap the benefits, but the costs are borne by individuals—people from many demographics and along the income scale, noting, "High housing prices force workers towards cheaper but less productive places."

Many of the projects in this book illustrate strategies for building tiny in urban areas. These approaches include urban infill, adaptive reuse, transforming and flexible living spaces, and microunit buildings and small lot developments that add density to an existing area. Drawn from cities across the globe, the houses, apartments, and multi-family buildings and developments make the most of constraints, as in the case of the narrow lots found in Poland or Japan, where a tight-knit urban fabric leaves only thin wedges of land. Townhouse-like houses like the Slim House in London or the House in Nada located in Kobe offer beautiful and airy living spaces on lots that present a host of challenges. The Slim House, designed by London-based architecture collective Alma-nac, for example, is a renovation and expansion of a nineteenth-century residence built in the old alley between two stately homes on the street.

The 150-square-foot Keret House in Warsaw by architect Jakub Szczęsny of the Warsaw-based firm Centrala is as much a skinny residence as it is an art project in the tradition of artist Gordon Matta-Clark's work *Fake Estates.* In 1973, Matta-Clark purchased from the City of New York microscaled and inaccessible parcels of land. He then photographed and mapped the fifteen sites to form the piece. Matta-Clark's artwork made commentary on the value of land in New York City during a bleak economic period for the city. He had bought the parcels in Queens and Staten Island for between twenty-five and seventy-five dollars each. Today, it is impossible to think of any scrap of urban land without wanting to immediately interpret its value. In Warsaw, the gap the house fills was the intersection between two

Nazi-era ghettos. Szczęsny's Keret House, just 48 inches wide, is the narrowest house in Warsaw. Squeezed between a pre–World War II tenement and a more contemporary apartment building, the project's value comes from making visible a piece of the city's history.

In Hong Kong, a city that has the highest population density in the world, with some areas reporting 400,000 people per square kilometer, tiny living is not simply an extreme sport, but a way of life. The impetus is to build better, not bigger. Edge Design Institute's Gary Chang took his own 344-square-foot studio apartment as a case study in how to construct a living unit that offers the spatial configurations and flexibility of a much larger abode. By designing moveable walls, transforming furniture, and hiding storage, as well as orchestrating the ballet of moving parts, he developed some twenty-four unique scenarios in a single space. The architect's twenty-four-room apartment is in the same physical location as the three-bedroom apartment he's lived in since he was fourteen, but his redesign pushes the functionality of the small space to the outer limits of possibilities. It illustrates how good design has the capability of enhancing and, in a way, enlarging the architectural experience.

Included in this volume are a few projects that are not tiny, but instead are thoughtful small houses and housing developments. These modest single-family residences make no claims to cuteness as their primary attribute, yet they represent urban strategies that follow in the tradition of the tiny house movement and are mindful of making the most out of a given situation. There's attention to reusing existing buildings, as in the case of the Flower House by Ezzo. In a city like Porto, Portugal, where the historical urban fabric is tightly knit, the architects renovated an old, dark masonry house into a light-filled 1,291-square-foot space. In Los Angeles, two small lot developments, Buzz Court by Heyday Partnership and Blackbirds by Bestor Architecture, suggest new typologies for housing. (L.A.'s Small Lot Subdivision Ordinance was developed to encourage much-needed housing in the city by permitting multiple townhouses on lots below the minimum size for a typical housing development.) Each add density to neighborhoods where housing is in high demand, but they do so with a sensitivity to building a community and sustainably responding to the landscape.

On the flip side, a Bia Hoi, a seven-story bike skyscraper by Swiss architecture firm Bureau A, is a mere 71 square feet. It is more of a sketch than a structure, but as a gesture about how to live in a city like Hanoi, it encapsulates the tiny ethos for efficiency and mobility. It also reminds us that city life is about engaging with the street, the neighborhood, in all its gritty glory. Ultimately, a bike skyscraper pedaling through boulevards and alleys presents urbanity as not a dark or scary experience, but as something joyous. Indeed, the tiny and small houses in this collection form an architectural act of celebration—a toast to many cities from a Brooklyn rooftop.

Bia Hoi for Ta di Ôtô

Bureau A
HANOI, VIETNAM
2013

Bia Hoi by Swiss architecture firm Bureau A is a blue bike skyscraper—a seven-story mobile structure mounted on a tricycle—commissioned by Ta đi Ôtô, a local bar and cultural center. The project, made from a framework of blue-painted steel tubes and designed to be ridden around the streets of Hanoi, is many things according to the architects: an ephemeral house, a vertical restaurant on wheels, an art installation, a micro–concert hall. As such, it's a stretch to categorize the project as a tiny house, per se, but given the rise of bicycle culture in U.S. cities, combined with increased density in urban areas, the mobile, microstructure is perhaps a vision of future housing.

Architects Leopold Banchini and Daniel Zamarbide drew inspiration directly from the urban fabric and the creativity of everyday Vietnamese life. "Everything is dense in Hanoi, including the milk in your coffee," they write, describing the project. "Everything is used. In unexpected ways 'things' live different lives, they reincarnate continuously into new functions, passing from one life to another without a moment of respite." Appropriately, the design adapts a tricycle owned by the steelworker who helped construct the mobile structure. The bike frame was expanded and reinforced to support the seven floors, each level configured for maximum use. The ground floor affords enough space to set up a cooking area. Sleeping, hanging out, and dining take place on the narrow platforms above. A small PVC roof crowns the tower, which is fitted out with a battery-powered fan and lights. Built in the outskirts of town, the bike skyscraper was ridden into the center of Hanoi—precariously dodging trucks and motorscooters—for a party at Ta đi Ôtô.

Chambre de Bonne

Kitoko Studio
PARIS, FRANCE
2014

Stately edifices line the boulevards of Paris. Behind the nineteenth-century stone facades are the grand, well-appointed apartments that housed the city's bourgeoisie. Tucked under the mansard roofs, however, are the cramped and secluded rooms that were once home to the servants. Over time, these spaces were abandoned or used for storage. Today, given the demand for real estate in the center of Paris, these rooms are up for reconsideration. Architect Gaylor Lasa Zingui and interior designer Morgane Guimbault of Kitoko Studio renovated an existing maid's room on the seventh floor of a Haussmann-era building into a cleverly efficient apartment that overlooks the rooftops.

The existing maid's room was rudimentary: a door, a window, a sink, and just enough room for a bed and wardrobe. The designers set about to create a fully functioning apartment, including a kitchenette and bathroom with shower. They refer to their concept as a Swiss Army knife approach. A big window lets light into the space and under it is a two-door cabinet that conceals the kitchenette: a small refrigerator, sink, and microwave. To maximize workspace for cooking, a counter surface folds down over the sink.

Dominating the room is a seemingly simple set of cabinets. A domestic wunderkammer, it opens up and unfolds to reveal everything needed to sleep, cook, work, and bathe. One cabinet reveals a shelving unit on castors that doubles as a set of steps to reach the loft bed hidden behind a sliding panel. Doors hide a wardrobe and more storage. A table and two chairs wheel out from behind another door and into the open area of the apartment. The bathroom door is integrated into the cabinetry. Inside the small chamber is a toilet, shower, and small sink. Fully tiled in a contemporary pattern with a drain in the floor, the bathroom is efficient but not uncomfortable.

Songpa Micro Housing

Single Speed Design (SsD)
SEOUL, KOREA
2014

Songpa Micro Housing, a mixed-use apartment building in Seoul, responds to increased urban density in the city, but also to cultural changes in Korea. Traditionally, young singles would live at home with their parents before marriage, leaving the family to form their own, but over the last decade there has been a rise in single and couple households. As such, there is increased demand for small, affordable housing options. Architects Jinhee Park and John Hong of the New York City and Seoul firm Single Speed Design (SsD) recognized the need to build apartments to fill the demand, but were cautious. They didn't want microhousing to be seen as temporary or disposable.

Their design is flexible, offering up a modular, 120-square-foot unit that can be combined and reconfigured by adding neighboring units as more space is needed. Each cement-paneled unit fits within a structural steel frame, which is wrapped with an expressive twisted, stainless-steel facade to provide privacy and shade. The facade, made out of 0.13-inch-thick flat bars, takes on various functions, twisting to become railings, trellises, and bike racks.

Inside, the white-walled prefabricated units include space-saving elements such as Murphy beds, lots of storage, and pull-out tables. Each unit is configured slightly differently, but in each clerestory windows seem to lift the ceiling, making the apartments feel more spacious. Balconies and small porches extend the living areas.

The whole building is 5,500 square feet. Within that volume is a wealth of urban-minded programs: a ground-floor café and micro-auditorium, a gallery, parking, and housing. Park and Hong dubbed the corridors and shared public areas between units as "tapioca space."

"If you look at a tapioca pearl, there's gel around it. And with a lot of microhousing, you have the corridor and then you have the housing," explained Hong in an interview with *Metropolis* magazine. "But we're focused on the kind of 'gel' around the unit that's semi-public—the shared corridors and balconies." The common areas are pleasant places for residents to gather and offer a way to extend their lives outside of the tiny apartments. The architects designed these tapioca spaces with the same considerations as they took to the apartments; there is good ventilation and natural light, even views out over the street.

Quixote Village

MSGS Architects
OLYMPIA, WA
2013

A collection of thirty 144-square-foot cottages laid out in a horseshoe on just over 2 acres, Quixote Village is more than an exercise in tiny living, it's a demonstration of using microhomes to build a community. The project, designed by Garner Miller of the Olympia-based firm MSGS Architects, is the permanent home to members of a homeless community called Camp Quixote.

Founded in 2007, the roving tent city was in need of a place to finally stake down roots. The group is a self-governing community that was searching for a different kind of shelter than a group home or apartment. As the residents settled into their new homes in 2013, the self-government evolved into the Village Resident Council, which represents through elected leaders the thirty men and women who live at Quixote Village. The nonprofit organization Panza supports the village and is the legal landlord and owner of the property.

The choice to build tiny houses was as much about economics as it was about finding a design that suited an itinerant group. The cost of the cottages, just half the size of micro-unit apartments planned for New York City, came in at just over half of the cost of a single affordable housing unit.

For the formerly homeless residents, the tiny cottages split the difference between autonomy and collective living. The cottages are arranged around a common green space. Each one includes a living space, water closet, and space for an individual vegetable garden. The design of the units is simple, a sketch of a miniature home with a storybook peaked roof over a porch. Yet the sitting porches are an important buffer zone between public and private space. A community building extends services, with a dining room, large kitchen, laundry, showers, offices, and community space.

Keret House

Centrala
WARSAW, POLAND
2012

Keret House is the narrowest house in Warsaw. It is also an art installation, a political statement, and a smart piece of architecture. Designed by architect Jakub Szczęsny of the Warsaw-based firm Centrala, the residence fits in the crack between two buildings on Żelazna Street, a space that at its widest is just under 5 feet. On one side is a pre–World War II tenement and on the other is more a contemporary cooperative apartment block. The gap between the two carries a deep history: it was the intersection between two Nazi-era ghettos.

Szczęsny first conceived of the project for the WolaArt festival in 2009, and it was developed into a residence and workspace for the Israeli writer Etgar Keret with the support of the nonprofit Polish Modern Art Foundation. Because of its narrowness—interior dimensions range from 48 inches at the widest to a mere 28 inches—the house is classified as an art installation not a residence, but it still offers the comforts of home.

Inside, a triangular truss supported by steel columns organizes and dominates the space. Insulated panels form the barrier between the structure and the adjacent buildings, while two narrow facades and the roof are clad in translucent polycarbonate panels. The translucent panels allow indirect light to filter into tight living quarters. Windows on each end allow for cross-ventilation.

The design challenges conventions of how you move through a building. The Keret House has no traditional front door. Instead, visitors walk up a short flight of stairs and pop through a trapdoor in the floor of the first level. The small space includes a kitchenette (with a sink, stove, and refrigerator), a dining area (two built-in seats and a little table), and a bathroom inspired by aircraft toilets. A metal ladder welded to the structure leads to a mezzanine and the sleeping and work areas. A mattress squeezed between the two walls gives new meaning to the phrase "sleep tight."

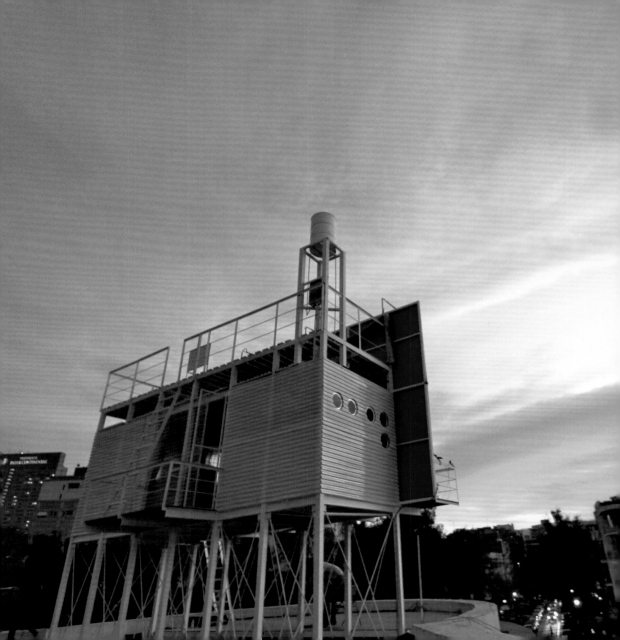

The Billboard House

Julio Gómez Trevilla
MEXICO CITY, MEXICO
2013

Mexico City is one of the densest megalopolises in Latin America. Several architects in the city take advantage of this condition by looking skyward and building penthouses or terraces on top of existing buildings. The Billboard House, designed by architect Julio Gómez Trevilla, is a play on that trend, an advertising stunt, and a legitimately tiny house. The small, temporary residence perched on top of a two-story building in Polanco, an upscale neighborhood west of the city center, is a study in how the tiny house movement might seek out opportunistic sites within urban areas.

The project was commissioned by an advertising agency as part of a campaign for the Mexican paper company Scribe. A steel structure raises the house 27 feet above the roof, and the street-facing side of the house acts as a billboard. Constraints of the campaign dictated that the design fit within a tight budget, be quickly assembled and disassembled, and, importantly, be livable. Mexican-born artist Cecilia Beaven lived in the house for ten days as she hand-painted a mural on the billboard.

A wooden walkway on the front of the Billboard House doubles as a front porch and a work platform for painting the mural. The front door is concealed in the billboard. Inside, Trevilla outfitted the house with a kitchenette, dressing room, closet, toilet-shower, and desk. Water for the sink and bath comes from a small tank mounted on a tower, which rises above the roof—adding even more quirk to the skyline. Although the walls and furniture are made out of off-the-shelf particleboard, the designer used bright accent colors—vibrant red, yellow, teal, and green—to playfully differentiate the areas. To give the artist a flexible workspace, Trevilla put the furniture on wheels, and the bed hinges up and out of the way when not in use.

To ensure maximum light inside the small living quarters Trevilla used translucent corrugated plastic sheeting on two sides of the structure. Porthole sized windows cut into the shower wall ensure privacy and create a pop graphic on the exterior. Mindful of heat gain within the unit, he created a double-layer roof: a wooden deck placed 2 feet above the ceiling. Like almost everything in the Billboard House, it serves double duty. The platform shades and protects the house from the elements and is a dramatic outdoor space and stage (bands played during the campaign) overlooking the neighborhood.

A Cabin in a Loft

A Cabin in a Loft, two wooded structures tucked inside a larger industrial space, illustrates how the principles of living small apply at any scale. Designer Terri Chiao's approach is whimsical, drawing on fundamental ideas of home. Her scheme creates privacy in an open loft without sacrificing light, air, and views.

Located within a former textile factory in Bushwick, an industrial neighborhood in Brooklyn with a burgeoning art and food scene, the raw space needed two bedrooms to make it livable. But Chiao, who graduated from Columbia University in 2008 with an architecture degree, wasn't content to simply construct sheetrock walls. The cabins were inspired by the weekends she spent as a child in the mountains of North Georgia and Tennessee.

Chiao designed the cabins and built them with a crew of friends. Each one is outfitted with just enough storage and privacy for one person. Her room, an 88-square-foot cabin, is an iconic pitched-roof shelter made out of lauan plywood and standard lumber. Spartan, it fits little more than a double bed. The raised floor provides storage space. Originally designed as a bedroom, it's now used as an office by Chiao and her partner, Adam Frezza.

The second cabin, a 100-square-foot plywood "treehouse," is raised 6 feet off the floor to accommodate a study and storage area. Picturesque windows cut into both cabins capture the southeastern light that floods the loft during the day and provide ventilation. Between the two structures, a 12-foot-tall, airy living room is filled with books and plants. "I like feeling connected to the weather, and in this space, the sun and the sky can be experienced pretty directly at all times through the big windows—so sometimes it does feel a little bit like I'm living outdoors," Chiao explains. "Maybe as close I can get to doing that comfortably in New York City anyway."

Miller House

Macy Miller
BOISE, ID
2011

In 2011, when designer Macy Miller embarked on building her own tiny house on the bed of a 24-foot-long, 8-foot-wide flatbed trailer she wasn't looking to embody a movement. Her life was turned upside down and she faced foreclosure on a 2,500-square-foot house. She simply needed to downsize. As an intern architect at a firm in Boise, Idaho, she saw constructing her own house as a chance to build her skills as well as a good financial proposition. She gave herself a budget of one year's rent and all her own labor, with the total adding up to be just over $11,000. The result is a long and narrow house that fits a couple, an infant, and even her Great Dane.

Located on a residential lot in downtown Boise, the house sits on a flatbed trailer for two reasons: First, mobility—Miller hopes to one day have the house operate off-grid. And second, building codes. According to Miller the city has a 600-square-foot minimum square footage for dwellings. In order to live small, she had to work around the existing code by building on a mobile structure. The trailer bed, however, created its own challenges. To install radiant floor heating she had to add a third axle to support the thermal mass—a 6,000-pound tile system on top of an inch and a half of mortar—and hand drill 180 holes through the steel frame. The exterior is clad in boards salvaged from recycled pallets, which Miller painstakingly collected, disassembled, and cut to fit.

Inside is just as meticulous: There's no wasted space. The front porch enters onto a narrow kitchen that fits a four-burner gas stove recycled from an old camper, a microwave, a full-size refrigerator, and a combined washer/dryer. Opposite, the small bathroom includes a tiny sink, tiled shower, and a composting toilet. Wherever possible, Miller created storage: hidden cabinets, built-in bookshelves, and a pantry. She elevated the bed, so there was just enough clearance under the sloped roof for a mattress, and added cupboards underneath and storage in the steps leading up to the bed. Comfortable upholstered armchairs in the living room might seem like a luxury when space is at a minimum; however, they're offset by a dining table that folds down when not in use.

Briefcase House

Bureau Spectacular
CHICAGO, IL
2010

Jimenez Lai takes a conceptual approach to how to live in micro architecture. Faced with a large, but undistinguished 1,400-square-foot live/work loft, he sought to test what it means to have your life and your material possessions inside a single, small space. His Briefcase House, named after the efficiency and portability of the attaché case, is as much a piece of cabinetry as it is a living unit.

The design takes inspiration from Mies van der Rohe's Farnsworth House, a one-room International Style cottage in Plano, Illinois. In the iconic, mid-century house, the modernist architect reduced the residence down to essentials: shelter and view. All the services—bathroom, kitchen, and storage—are compacted inside a streamlined piece of teak cabinetry in the middle the all-glass house. By creating a domestic unit in his warehouse loft, Lai pays homage but also reverses the program uses. His Briefcase House holds a bed, storage, seating areas, a closet, and a library, while the kitchen and the bathroom are part of the warehouse's larger space, which he uses as his office.

As a house within a house, Lai's design frustrates expressions of domesticity. The living and sleeping quarters are built out of spare, unfinished plywood, and the entire unit sits on castors, so that it can be rolled and reconfigured within the larger space. When the Briefcase House is not in use, a series of folding doors can be closed to ensure privacy, transforming the domestic unit into a wooden box floating in the loft.

Minim House

Foundry Architects
WASHINGTON, D.C.
2013

In 2013, Brian Levy commissioned Foundry Architects to design a prototype for micro living. Although interested in and supportive of the tiny house movement, he was critical of the cabin-like designs that had come to define the trend. Small windows let in diminished light. The go-to space-saving techniques of lofts and built-ins made the little spaces feel cramped. He looked to contemporary design as a precedent for a spacious interior and a streamlined exterior. The result is the 210-square-foot Minim House, which combines a modern approach with sustainable features such as a solar energy system powered by an array of photovoltaic cells for off-grid power, a rainwater harvesting system, and finishes and fabrics made from low off-gassing materials.

Levy and Foundry Architects worked with Element Design+Build on the construction of the Minim prototype, which is located on a plot of land owned by Levy in Washington, D.C., called the Micro Showcase. True to its name, the showcase offers a variety of ways to address small-space living. Minim shares the showcase with tiny homes grouped around a central outdoor common area, including

a studio that is a retrofit of a shipping container and a small house built by students at Washington, D.C.'s Academy of Construction and Design.

Constructed on top of a trailer, the 11-foot-wide-by-22-foot-long Minim House is slightly wider than many trailer-based tiny homes and is considered a wide load for towing. For Levy, the extra hassle of a wide load is worth it for the additional interior space. The width allowed him place the kitchen across the short end of the house, with the bathroom, office, and roll-away bed fitting neatly on the other end. In between the two is a generous living area defined by a low-slung, couch-like banquette (which also doubles as a guest bed). The sofa seat lifts for access to storage and a water tank and filtration system. A multifunctional table is one of many of the project's design innovations. Metal sockets are placed strategically around the house to offer different table configurations. The moveable table, built out of marine hardware, can be used as a dining table, a low coffee table, added counter space in the kitchen, as a bar, or as a desk that faces out the window.

Studio for an Artist

Raanan Stern
TEL AVIV, ISRAEL
2014

How do you fit eight decades of personal and family history into 215 square feet? Israeli architects Raanan Stern and Shany Tal answer the question with a compact design for an artist's studio that serves various functions: it's a workspace, an archive, and even a place to sleep. Located in an existing concrete 1950s apartment building in central Tel Aviv, the scheme accommodates a collection of print materials dating back to 1940. Two large windows hung with sheer white curtains let diffuse sunlight into the room.

The proper sorting and storage of these books, prints, and papers are as important as the quality of light and material character in this small space, which includes two desks, 36 drawers, multiple modular storage compartments, and a pegboard for the display of books and ephemera. Stern and Tal began their design process by measuring every piece of the collection over the course of four weeks. The artifacts were then organized into groupings according to size and subject. During this research phase, they identified four distinct proportions, which then guided the design of the white birch storage walls. Every cell, cupboard, or drawer is specific to a kind of paper or object. However, the exact category does not immediately register in the space. "During measuring we gave each category a color, which is exposed only when one opens a drawer or any other unit," said Stern in an interview with the design website Dezeen.

Color is not the only surprise. A birch pegboard, used to display artifacts, slides to reveal a folding bed, which the artist uses to host guests. Additionally, some sliding wall pieces can be removed to double as modular easels. The smaller drawers, color-coded in light blue, can be removed from the shelf and placed on the table for everyday use.

Amalgro Apartment

MYCC
MADRID, SPAIN
2012

For many architects, the plan is the most-used drawing for design. It affords a magical bird's-eye view of all the rooms. But for tiny dwellings, where maximizing square footage is the prime concern, it is a different architectural drawing, the section, which is the best for visualizing an efficient design. A sectional understanding of a volume is great for creating stacked spaces and hidden layers. Faced with a renovation of a skinny, box-like apartment in Madrid, architects Carmina Casajuana, Beatriz G. Casares, and Marcos Gonzalez of the Spanish firm MYCC took advantage of 16-foot-tall ceilings in the unit to develop distinct living, sleeping, and eating spaces along the longitudinal section.

Designed for photographer Elena Almagro, the scheme uses level changes rather than walls to distinguish each room. Entry into the apartment happens on the second floor. One step up leads to the kitchen and then a short flight of stairs descends into the living room. From there a ladder attached to the wall leads to an office area. More private spaces are placed lower in the volume. Tucked under the mezzanine is the bedroom, reached by three stairs, and the bathroom (with a luxurious *hammam* bath) is hidden under the entry foyer. A trap door in the living room reveals a crawlspace with plenty of underfloor storage.

Daylight enters the apartment from a large operable skylight above the mezzanine office. Its brightness draws the eye upward and emphasizes the overall height of the apartment. In addition, constantly moving up and down and through the apartment gives the space an expansiveness it would otherwise lack: views within the all-white space change as the light changes, and the exertion of climbing rungs or stairs amplifies the physical engagement with each room.

Domestic Transformer

EDGE Design Institute Ltd.
HONG KONG, CHINA
2008

Architect Gary Chang of EDGE Design Institute has lived in his Hong Kong apartment since he was fourteen. For more than thirty years, Chang has taken inspiration for research and design from the 344-square-foot unit, one of 370 in a 17-story apartment building. When he lived there as a teenager with his parents and sisters, the space was divided up into three tiny bedrooms, a kitchen, and a hallway.

Later, after he bought the apartment, he removed all the partitions and divided the one large space with curtains. In 2008, Chang was working through principles of how to improve compact living, given the huge demand for housing in Hong Kong. Using his own home as a prototype, he created what he calls the Domestic Transformer, a living space that transforms the tight space into twenty-four different "rooms." He explains that his design is "an experiment in putting all the essential and unexpected activities into this compact space without compromise."

The apartment has an otherworldly feel, due primarily to the yellow-tinted scrim on the window, and also because nothing is what it seems. Wall units move to reveal other spaces, such as the kitchen or wet bar. Steel ceiling-mounted tracks support the cabinetry, leaving it hovering above a polished granite floor. These units contain a host of adaptable furniture such as a fold-down couch, a double hydraulic Murphy bed, worktables, seating, and even a hammock. Shelves lining the party walls house Chang's extensive CD collection. Chang has categorized each possible living variation, naming some two dozen possible configurations such as TV Game, Guest Bedroom, Maximum Kitchen, and Yoga. The Home Spa arrangement proves one of the biggest surprises—push the walls aside and you'll find an all-glass shower that doubles as a steam room and, most unexpectedly for such a tiny space, a luxurious, full-size bathtub.

Drs. Julian and Raye Richardson Apartments

David Baker and Associates
SAN FRANCISCO, CA
2011

Richardson Apartments, designed by David Baker and Associates, is located in San Francisco's Hayes Valley, a neighborhood central to public transportation that had suffered from twin pressures, first from blight after the demolition of a piece of freeway following the Loma Prieta earthquake, and then from swift economic changes that threatened affordability. Commissioned by the Community Housing Partnership and Mercy Housing California, Richardson is home to very low-income, formerly homeless residents. In a region where the tech boom is driving up demand for housing and consequently prices, Richardson is part of a long-term effort to build affordable housing throughout the city. The project demonstrates how an infill development of 120 microunits can both help stabilize the urban fabric and the lives of San Francisco's neediest citizens.

Life in the five-story building centers on the landscaped courtyard, off of which are resident services, including a medical clinic, counseling center, lounge areas, and a social-enterprise corner bakery. Built-in benches, large tables, and planters make it a welcoming space to hang out. Part of the success of the courtyard is due to the fact that there is no on-site parking. The transit-minded design favors pedestrians and bikes over cars.

A large exterior staircase connects the four upper levels of studio apartments. The architects designed balcony-like landings to foster interaction between residents and lighten the load on the elevator in the lobby. Although the microunits are densely packed together along corridors, inside they are bright and efficient. Typical units are 345 square feet and are equipped with a kitchen and full bathroom. Generous operable windows fill the units with light and air. Residents also have access to a deck on the green roof, which offers a place for urban agriculture as well as sweeping views of the San Francisco skyline.

Sanchez Residence

Good Idea Studio
CULVER CITY, CA
2014

Culver City, considered part of greater Los Angeles, sprung up in the 1920s, when unassuming bungalows were built to serve nearby centers of industry, including Hughes Aircraft Company and Hollywood studios such as Metro-Goldwyn-Mayer. It was an urban fabric composed of workers housing—the American Dream on a small scale, two bedroom homes on modest lots with trim front lawns and a backyard. Today, Culver City is part of Silicon Beach, the growing center of L.A.'s tech industry, and is becoming increasingly desirable for its connectivity to public transportation and walkable neighborhoods.

The Sanchez Residence, designed by Louis Molina and Laurent Turin of the Los Angeles–based Good Idea Studio, is an in-law unit attached to an existing garage that sits behind a stucco bungalow. Molina and Turin's design increases on-site density and provides the client, Ellen Sanchez, with a flexible living area and a maximized outdoor space for lounging and dining. The architects took a playful take on the typical wood-frame structure. One wall of the little house cants inward and is clad in translucent polycarbonate panels. This gesture creates a triangular-shaped window on the facade and brings light into the interior while maintaining privacy.

Inside, the architects created a plywood jewel box. Sheets of plywood follow the folded profile of the roof and walls. The everyday material is also used to create a shelving system that wraps the space to make a screen for the shower. The all-wood interior hints at Los Angeles's modernist legacy, referencing the designs of Rudolph Schindler and the mid-century Case Study houses. But perhaps the plywood interior is most suggestive of the so-called Spruce Goose, the H-4 Hercules aircraft made out of laminated birch plywood at nearby Hughes Aircraft Company.

Tokyo Apartment

Sou Fujimoto Architects
TOKYO, JAPAN
2010

"This collective housing is the miniature of Tokyo—a Tokyo which never exists is made into a form," writes Japanese architect Sou Fujimoto, describing the whimsical Tokyo Apartment. His design, located in a residential neighborhood in the center of Tokyo, is meant to capture the spirit of the crowded and chaotic city. The four-apartment project is made of up stacked "houses"—iconically shaped rooms stacked on top of each other to form a seemingly precarious tower. It's a somewhat literal interpretation of life in an ever-densifying urban environment.

Each unit is made up of two or three rooms interconnected by an equally jumbled collection of stairways and ladders. The interiors of the two- and three-room units range from roughly 450 to 600 square feet. While the most practical rooms—the bathrooms and kitchens—are carefully de-fined, other spaces such as living rooms and bedrooms are left undefined, flexible to meet the individual needs of the residents. Instead of catering to function, the all-white apartments show the traces of the units perched above or below: columns skewer through rooms, and the ceilings and floors are punctuated with openings to let in light or lead to other spaces.

The exterior stairwells act as a kind of social mixer. Residents have rooms at both the bottom and the top of the building, and so are often passing each other on the way up or down. Fujimoto poetically compares the wood-frame structure to a mountain, and a mountain to the whole of city of Tokyo. "When you go up the outside stairs, you will have the experience of climbing a big mountain such as a city," he notes. "Your house is at the foot and summit of a mountain."

Unfolding Apartment

Michael K. Chen Architecture
NEW YORK, NY
2007

In Manhattan, where living in small spaces is the stuff of punch lines, organizing a tiny apartment is something of an extreme sport. New York City–based architect Michael Chen has made something of a specialty out of the compact: he's designed several small and flexible apartments in New York, including the 420-square-foot Unfolding Apartment, on which he collaborated with Kari Anderson. "Bigger than furniture, smaller than architecture," says Chen of his approach.

Rather than trying to disguise his intervention or match the existing architecture, Chen's designs draw attention. For his bachelor client, Eric Schneider, who uses his space for entertaining and working from home, Chen created a cobalt blue oversized cabinet. The custom piece is set against one wall

of the apartment, leaving room for a galley kitchen and the living room. All other functions are stored in or unfold from the tall cabinet: a Murphy bed (complete with nightstand), a closet, a fold-down office desk, a library, a pantry, and a bar. A lighting system is also built into the piece.

In addition to everything stashed away inside the big, blue bureau, a large screen on a castor pivots open to create a privacy barrier between the living room and the bedroom, needed when overnight guests stay on the fold-out couch in the living room. When all the elements from the cabinet are deployed, the studio is transformed from a single loft-like space into four distinct rooms.

Passage Buhan

Fabre/deMarien Architects
BORDEAUX, FRANCE
2009

In 2006, Bordeaux-based architects Julie Fabre and Matthieu de Marien converted a Chinese restaurant into a modest house: Ice Cube, which is included in this book. Their 2009 Passage Buhan house continues the firm's commitment to practicing a kind of urban alchemy, the transformation of existing building stock—commercial structures, storage depots, and factories—into renewed architectural environments. The 441-square-foot project adapted a run-down garage located in a cobblestone alley—the Passage Buhan, a lane dating back to the eighteenth century.

Hemmed in by party walls, the property's only facade faces the street, which left few options for windows into the residence. Fabre and de Marien were faced with the challenge of how to bring light into the modest space. They solved the problem by replacing the existing dilapidated garage door with a sliding pine facade that opens up to reveal an entry and teak-floored patio about the size of a parking space. In fact, the 95-square-foot patio is designed to double as

a parking spot to meet city regulations. Most of the time, however, it is used as an extended part of the living area. Large sliding glass doors surround outdoor space, letting sunlight into the kitchen and dining area.

Designed for Jérémie Buchholtz, the house caters to the needs of a bachelor photographer. In the living area, a multifunctional Douglas fir cube construction conceals a bathroom, the boiler, a washing machine, and a dressing room. At roughly 10 by 12 feet, the cube fills the space, but doesn't dominate. A sofa bed and office are cut into its side, lessening the bulk. A set of stairs on the back side of the cube leads to a sleeping area. To create privacy as well as gain enough head clearance, the bed is recessed into the top of the cube. Shelving and storage form a parapet around the tiny bedroom. The space is tight, but a skylight cut into the roof right above the bed provides morning light and frames the night sky.

All I Own House

PKMN architectures
MADRID, SPAIN
2014

Stuff. One of the most challenging aspects of tiny house living is how we deal with our stuff: the necessities and mementos of daily life. Often, scaling down to a smaller living space means shedding the belongings we hold so dear. The design for the All I Own House by PKMN architectures takes a generous approach to dealing with stuff. Collaborators Rocío Pina, David Pérez, Enrique Espinosa, and Carmelo Rodríguez recognize the emotional connection we have to our things and surroundings, writing: "Each of our possessions has its own private story, a memory associated to it and, just the same way in which we grow and change, our personal belongings change, we get rid of some stuff but we resist losing much of it, we could easily picture ourselves through our possessions."

The architects renovated a semi-detached, single-story house just north of Madrid that their client, Yolanda Pila, inherited from her grandmother. Although the 462-square-foot space space is small, the residence has a large garden with established plantings. Rather than expanding the interior with an addition, the architects maintained the connection between the inside and the outside with large, shuttered, floor-to-ceiling operable windows. Inside, they reckoned with stuff.

The interior is divided into two main areas: a 250-square-foot living area that is nearly devoid of all furniture except a large table, and the storage area, a series of movable plywood cabinets that are hung on rails mounted high on the wall. The cabinets hold and conceal everything from Pila's books, records, clothing, and cookware to her bedroom, which unfolds to reveal a full-size mattress and a side table. A bathroom and a streamlined kitchen bookend the movable cabinets, so that when the cabinets are positioned one way, a full kitchen and dining table emerges, while reconfiguring the cabinets another way finds an all-white bathroom, glass-enclosed shower, and dressing room. The house is flexible and adaptable based on time of day, function, and need for privacy, but it changes the paradigm of tiny: there's still plenty of room for stuff.

Oddo Studio

Good Idea Studio
LOS ANGELES, CA
2007

At just 495 square feet, the Oddo Studio is an exercise in scaling back without sacrificing livability. In 2002, John Oddo purchased a Victorian house dating from 1897 in Los Angeles's Echo Park neighborhood. The building, which had been damaged in a fire that destroyed the second floor, was a mishmash of lousy additions and making due. Initially, Oddo turned to Louis Molina and Laurent Turin of the L.A.–based practice Good Idea Studio to remodel and expand the house, but smack in the middle of the economic downturn he had difficulty getting a construction loan. Molina suggested that he build a smaller house, but one that maximizes the space and creates good connection between indoors and outdoors—a basic tenet of California design. The one-bedroom house, while not an expansion, feels expansive.

"It was important that the first impression wasn't small and cheap," Molina told the *Los Angeles Times*. "We didn't want it to look like we had to make compromises." The structure's street facade is simple—a stucco box, accented with just a single vertical window and a steel frame for climbing vines.

What seems like the front door is actually a steel and frosted acrylic gate that leads to an entry court. Entrance into the house is informal, through a glass door framed in Douglas fir, as are all the sliding doors and windows that line the perimeter of the living room and kitchen. There is a large dining table on the rear patio, shaded by a deep roof overhang. By treating outdoor spaces as an extension of the indoors, Molina casually grew the building footprint.

The south wall, which faces a neighboring property, is dedicated to function. It is embedded with a small kitchen and storage cabinets that extend from the living area into the bedroom. A bookcase conceals the bulk of the cube-like volume that contains the bathroom and additional storage. The bedroom, like the rest of the house, feels enlarged due to the outdoor space. Floor-to-ceiling glass doors open out onto a private courtyard. Although pale blue stucco walls insulate the intimate space from the street, there is no roof, just a view of the sky.

White Hut and Tilia Japonica

Takahashi Maki and Associates

SAITAMA, JAPAN

2010

The White Hut and Tilia Japonica is a small house that tells a natural history of its site. Located in a residential neighborhood of Saitama, an area that was once rice fields, the design by architects Takahashi Maki and Shiokami Daisuke of the Tokyo-based firm Takahashi Maki and Associates pays homage to the site's past river-delta landscape. Before a spate of nondescript, blocky houses cropped up in the 1960s, there was once a stream—a distributary of the nearby Arakawa River—running through the area. The architects chose building materials and landscaping that reference the waterway: gravel to recall the riverbed and live trees that are native to waterfronts, the *Cercidiphyllum japonicum* and the *Tilia japonica*. Inside, timber from the latter species is used as shelving.

Life in the house, a tall, narrow structure, takes place across three floors tucked behind a symmetrical, white metal facade that is topped by a pitched roof. The first floor, which is raised to account for historic flood levels, houses a small entryway and, in an unusual arrangement, the bedroom and a work area. The stair is built like a piece of cabinetry. It hides a small water closet and plenty of storage. The second floor houses a kitchen and living area. In order to give a lightness to the space, the architects created a pair of windows that run from the first to the third floors. The stairwell occupies this thin slot of space on one side, but on the opposite side it is a triple-height void that enhances the interior.

The stairwell continues to the third floor, which is dedicated to ablutions. A large soaking tub fills the space, and light pours through the glass window that follows the line of the truss roof. For privacy, the architects provided a curtain on a curved track to block the tub and toilet from the adjacent dressing area and stairwell. On each floor the walls are lined with shelves made from *Tilia japonica*, the soft, lightweight wood from the lime tree family. The shelving, filled with books, dishware, and wicker baskets, is the backdrop for life in the White Hut.

House in Rokko

Fujiwara-Muro Architects
KOBE, JAPAN
2012

The House in Rokko, designed by architects Shintaro Fujiwara and Yoshio Muro, presents an unusual design approach to small living. Where some designers opt for opening up and decluttering the experience of the house, Fujiwara and Muro complicate and obscure the interior. Even from the street there is something off-kilter about the small house in a residential neighborhood in Kobe. The roof pitches dramatically and the facade angles sharply back from the street. (The angle makes room for a driveway and a covered entry vestibule.)

The property is just 13 feet wide and 50 feet long, so the critical question the architects asked themselves was how to get sunlight into a long and narrow site. A large window on the front facade was not possible, but an answer came from the desires of the client, who expressed interest in the atmosphere of mountain cabins and wooden huts. The scheme divides the house into two little huts, one at the front and one at the back of the property. One contains the bathroom and kitchen, the other living and sleeping quarters. Further emphasizing the cabin-like feel, both are finished entirely in wood panels.

Between the huts is a kind of "outdoor" room—a double-height space lit from a large skylight. Short flights of stairs connect each of the program areas, so that an occupant is always crossing through the middle zone, with a TV lounge tucked under one of the ground-floor staircases. Although the stairs might at first seem redundant, the result is a series of views across the house that change from dark to bright to dark again, making the spaces seem dynamic and, in turn, enlarges the feel of the home. The acute angle from the facade is repeated on the interior, which heightens the interplay between light, texture, and form.

House in Nada

Fujiwara-Muro Architects
KOBE, JAPAN
2012

Narrow houses on tight urban lots present a singular challenge: how to get light deep into the center of the house. Faced with a site about as wide as a parking space, architects Shintaro Fujiwara and Yoshio Muro needed to create a home that included all the basics for a family of four. Their solution: stack the spaces—a parking spot, bathroom, a bright living room, two rooms for the children, a master bedroom—on three floors while providing an innovative light well at the center of the structure.

Behind the spare, red-cedar facade the entry sequence to the house is unconventional. After squeezing by a parked car and entering a small foyer, visitors are greeted by a view of the family bathtub. In fact, the entire first floor is dedicated to bathing. In addition to the glass-enclosed tub, there's a water closet and a washroom. The solution is both intimate and functional. The entrance hall floor is made out of wood slats and fitted with an under-floor drain so that children and adults can splash a bit in the tub.

A tight run of steps leads to the second floor. The design efficiently houses a dining room, galley kitchen, and living room on a single floor, but it doesn't feel cramped. A sense of spaciousness comes from several critical design decisions: first, integrated shelving that runs from the kitchen to the living room and expands the space horizontally while creating much-needed storage. Second, the living area is sunken, giving it a unique spatial quality and more headroom. And third, a two-story light well brings air and daylight deep into the heart of the house. Topped with a large, operable skylight, it creates a micro-atrium. Slats in the floor allow daylight to filter into the entry hall below. The architects selected a glass-topped dining table as not to obscure the light.

Sleeping quarters on the third floor maximize as much space as possible. A curtain divides the master bedroom from the hallway. The children's bedrooms are one of the biggest surprises of House in Nada. The floor area in each room is only 34 square feet, but by creating a novel bunk bed the architects were able to stack sleeping areas. One room has access to the lower bunk and the other to the upper bunk. It is the architects' attention to details, like a built-in laundry line hung across the atrium and a ladder to the roof deck, that makes the place feel like home.

Salva46

Miel Arquitectos and Studio P10
BARCELONA, SPAIN
2014

Co-housing, the idea of intentional community-building around a set of common principles and common spaces, dates back to the 1980s. These kinds of homes often manifest as a series of small, freestanding residential structures grouped around a main public space. But what happens when collective living merges with an urban environment and apartment living?

That was the question taken up by Miel Arquitectos and Studio P10 in their design for Salva46. An experiment in what the architects call "shared micro-living," the apartment houses two units in one 700-square-foot structure. Unlike a roommate situation, which brings together friends or strangers under one roof, Salva46 is composed of two distinct apartments, each with individual areas for sleeping, working, relaxing, and bathing. Residents share a central kitchen and dining area.

The architects approached the project with attention to what is private and what is communal. The design allows each resident to modulate how much interaction they want to engage in. The front door enters directly into the central common cooking and dining areas in the middle of the long apartment. Although modest in size, the central space is more generous than the individual units because it is shared between the residents. Features include a full-size stove, refrigerator, and a built-in wine rack and pantry.

The all-white spaces are bright and airy, with high ceilings. Throughout the two units, the architects preserved original tiles and wooden beams, adding character and texture to the space. Light and ventilation was especially important to the design. Each unit can be independently secured without losing the light that spills in the large windows on each side of the building. The 11-foot-high ceilings throughout the apartment allowed the designers to maximize living space by inserting small mezzanines or platforms for use as combination library/lounge areas, which are strategically located over the beds.

Urban Post-Disaster Housing Prototype

Garrison Architects
NEW YORK, NY
2014

In the wake of the destruction wrought by Hurricane Sandy on the Eastern Seaboard in 2012, Garrison Architects developed a modular, post-disaster housing prototype for the New York City Office of Emergency Management. Commissioned by American Manufactured Structures and Services, who were contracted by the U.S. Army Corps of Engineers, the design serves urban residents displaced by catastrophic events and can be set up in less than 15 hours.

FEMA trailer homes, commonly deployed as temporary housing, are onerous to adapt to dense urban areas. They require big swaths of land rarely available in cities. By contrast, the urban prototype developed by Garrison Architects is stackable and reconfigurable. They can be trucked into any number of sites: vacant lots, front yards, public plazas, craned into place, and connected to utilities. A separate steel stair assembly provides access to the upper units.

"Aside from the basics of providing shelter after a disaster, the prototype is innovative because it allows residents to remain within their communities instead of being displaced for months, or even years," explains architect James Garrison. "'Shelter in place' allows residents to maintain their support networks—their friends and their families. Keeping neighborhoods intact is crucial for successful rebuilding."

Each home is small, just over 400 square feet for a one-bedroom to roughly 700 square feet for a three-bedroom apartment, yet it contains everything an individual or family would need to begin to rebuild their life post-disaster: a living area, bathroom, fully equipped kitchen, and storage space. The architects selected durable, recyclable materials such as cork flooring and formaldehyde-free finishes. Importantly, the steel shell is double-insulated, and the units can be equipped with photovoltaic panels for off-grid power.

W-Window House

Alphaville Architects
KYOTO, JAPAN
2012

Viewed from a narrow lane in Kyoto, the W-Window House is a cipher, a blank tower of metal siding with a sole door breaking up the severe facade. Yet for Kentaro Takeguchi and Asako Yamamoto of Kyoto-based Alphaville Architects, the residence, as per its name, is all about the windows. "We designed this space not only as a house but also as a three-dimensional window, a staircase, and a ventilation device," they explain.

The 3-D windows are two V-shaped indentations in the northeast and southwest facades. On the ground floor, these triangular divots form twin patios. Operable windows, 23 feet tall and set into the recess, serve every room: the two bedrooms, the living and dining rooms, and even the first-floor bath and utility rooms. Changing the building profile opened up the interior so that light—so key to tall and skinny

structures—can penetrate the house. The windows also promote air circulation via a chimney effect. Fresh air is drawn in at the bottom of the house and exhausted at the top.

The interior is composed of minimal, all-white walls with re-fined details. Visual complexity comes not from elaborate material choices but from how the spaces flow together. The architects built two stories in the front of the house and three in the rear. The misalignment or split-level construc-tion allowed for varying degrees of privacy and separation between the different programs with few partition walls. More public spaces such as kitchen and dining room are on the ground level and the living room is up one flight of stairs, while more intimate bedrooms are on the third and fourth floors. Exquisitely detailed stairs—steel sheets bent into risers and treads—seem to float as they lead from one level to another.

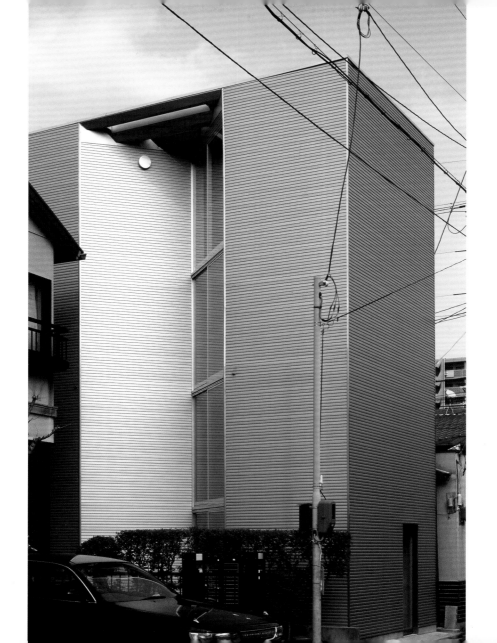

Ice Cube

Fabre/deMarien Architects
BORDEAUX, FRANCE
2006

Sometimes tiny living in urban environments means seeing residential potential in unlikely places. Bordeaux-based architects Julie Fabre and Matthieu de Marien did just that when they converted a former single-story Chinese restaurant located in a suburban Bordeaux neighborhood into an airy, two-story house.

Stripping out the old kitchen and tacky storefront, the architects adapted and retrofitted the existing structure, adding a steel and glass second story on top of the old concrete building. Because local building codes required an enclosed parking space, they modified the former storefront into a gated garage and entrance porch. Once inside, a steel spiral staircase leads to the loft-like second floor. Constructed out of a steel frame and corrugated steel cladding, Fabre and de Marien designed the addition to be lightweight enough

to sit on top of the existing concrete slab roof. The original parapets are visible inside the living space.

Upstairs, the exposed structure and cladding, as well as an unfinished plywood floor, convey an industrial aesthetic, yet the home is bright and welcoming. A long ribbon window set into the facade frames a cinematic view of the street. The U-shaped living space is centered on a central patio. Floor-to-ceiling steel and glass windows surrounding the patio let light and air into the living room and kitchen, as well as into the two modest bedrooms on the ground floor. The patio windows between the kitchen and living room endlessly frame and reframe daily life in the small home and they offer unique views of the neighboring rooftops—a collage of pitched tile, pressed metal, and glimpses of the sky.

Eel's Nest

Anonymous Architects
LOS ANGELES, CA
2011

The oft-told story of Los Angeles is that it is a sprawling megapolis, an endless suburb crisscrossed by freeways. The truth is that L.A. is stranger than that fiction. The urban fabric is both dense and loose. Eel's Nest, the narrow two-bedroom house designed by architect Simon Storey, is located in Echo Park, an L.A. neighborhood where older bungalows and newer developments are squeezed along hilly streets. The name of the house comes from the Japanese term for very narrow lots, and at 15 feet wide the residence lives up to the moniker. However, it replaces an even tinier house—a 370-square-foot structure dating from 1927 that Storey lived in prior to designing his own home.

The architect's compact scheme takes advantage of the sloped hillside. Storey kept the footprint of the garage, reinforcing and upgrading the walls, then stacked two floors on top. The first floor, reached by a stair attached to the garage, houses the living room and modest kitchen. Large windows on the front of the house overlook the street and let light deep into the interior. Sliding glass doors at the back open onto a small patio, visually extending the living and dining areas into the garden. Free of partition walls, the space feels more expansive than its square footage. To keep this sense of openness, the stair leading to the second floor is left unenclosed. White, floor-to-ceiling balusters reinforce the house's vertical flow of spaces.

The stairway leads to the bedrooms on the second floor, which share a bathroom lit by a skylight. As on the first floor, generous, wall-sized windows expand the interior spaces outward. In the rear bedroom, Storey covered three walls in black, flocked wallpaper, which helps directs the eye toward the view while maintaining a sense of intimacy. Storey uses the front bedroom as his office. From his desk he gazes over the neighborhood—the view is almost cinematic. Every part of the house is maximized for use. A roof deck with built-in seating offers a space to gaze at the Hollywood sign, the stars, and the San Gabriel Mountains.

Slim House

Alma-nac Collaborative Architecture
LONDON, UNITED KINGDOM
2012

True to its name, the Slim House by Caspar Rodgers, Chris Bryant, and Tristan Wigfall of the London-based architecture collective Alma-nac, is a slender seven and a half feet wide. The project is a renovation and expansion of an existing terrace house—a house that constituted an early urban infill. The original nineteenth-century residence was built in an old alley that led to rear stables behind the more stately houses on the street.

Hemmed in by buildings on either side that over the years had grown and extended to nearly encompass the lot, the house no longer received much natural light and felt cramped, with bedrooms facing a noisy street. The architects, working within a tight budget, created a design that kept the existing facade, but reworked the entire back of the structure and created a continuous, slate-clad sloped roof. Multiple skylights are strategically positioned to direct daylight into

the dining room, study, and master bedroom. Additionally, the architects positioned skylights over the central stairwell, which allows light to filter deep into the building.

On the ground floor, the architects created a long and narrow kitchen and dining room, which terminate in a set of oak-framed French doors that open directly onto the garden. Upstairs, the design maintained the original street-side bedroom on the second floor and expanding the third floor bedroom into a master suite. In order to maximize storage areas, the architects tucked a compact loft space over the upstairs bathroom and built a dressing area with freestanding closets, so as not to compromise the flood of light coming in from the skylights. Exposed brick throughout the house is a reminder of the structure's original condition, but warm wood and white plaster erase the old musty interior. The space, although narrow, is bright and expansive.

Flower House

EZZO
PORTO, PORTUGAL
2013

The modest Flower House, a 1,291-square foot project by Porto-based architecture and graphic design firm Ezzo, illustrates the power of adaptive reuse in a dense urban fabric. Flower House is located in Porto's Foz Velha neighborhood, a historic district of the city where closely packed houses climb up the hill from the edge of the Douro River. Architect César Machado Moreira in collaboration with João Pedro Leal recognized the sensitivity of the site. The Flower House scheme responds to the particular scale, textures, and geometries of the area: tightly packed houses constructed out of stone and stucco and topped with sloped, red tile roofs. The designers renovated the ground floor, replacing a warren of cramped rooms with a single space for living, dining, and cooking. They demolished and rebuilt the second story, keeping within the size of the original. Clad entirely in white stucco with light-colored tiles on the roof, the house distinguishes itself through color, not gesture.

The entrance to the house is just off a narrow alley but, once in the front door, the house becomes both sculptural and expansive. A thick, polished concrete floor stretches from the entry to a rear courtyard. The designers treated it as malleable surfaces, carving out recessed areas for the kitchen and a sunken living room, each reached by a few steps. By sinking programs into the floor, the space feels taller and more varied. In the kitchen, cabinets tuck under the floor level and a lozenge-shaped piece of cantilevered concrete serves as additional counter space. A built-in couch and fireplace add comfort to the sunken living room.

A concrete stair, finished with wood risers, leads to the two upstairs bedrooms—a larger master suite and a narrow bedroom with just enough room for a twin bed. To maximize livable space, Moreira added a study under the rake of the roof. The attic-like space is reached by a ladder and lined with bookshelves. An operable window offers a view of the adjacent rooftops and the Douro beyond.

Townhouse

Elding Oscarson
LANDSKRONA, SWEDEN
2009

At just over 1,300 square feet, the Townhouse is not exactly tiny in the truest sense. However, the small structure is an elegant and efficient approach to urban infill. Just 15 feet wide, the roughly 800-square-foot lot is tucked between two older buildings on a cobblestone street in Landskrona, Sweden. By comparison, new home lots in the United States are often more than ten times that size, with surveys from that last few years reporting median lot areas at 8,000 to 15,000 square feet. The narrowness of the lot, combined with an economic dip in the region—Sweden's wharf industry crisis in the 1980s impacted the beach town—left the lot vacant for decades.

Stockholm-based architects Johan Oscarson and Jonas Elding approached the design with sensitivity to the scale of the urban fabric. While their stark-white townhouse sits in contrast to the low adjacent structures, the overall massing and height are consistent with the mix of nearby buildings. Minimal openings—an entry and two windows—repeat the size and proportion of the neighboring facades but not the decorative details.

A glass entry door leads from the street directly into the kitchen, which flows into the main gathering area of the house, a double-height space that looks out on the courtyard garden. The all-white house is almost entirely free of partition walls, with every room (even the upstairs master bathroom) open. The only walls are along the exterior perimeter. Oscarson and Elding achieved a rare combination of openness and privacy by staggering the floor plates—thin exposed steel slabs finished with spruce planks. The floors, not the walls, divide up the domestic areas: kitchen and dining on the ground level; living room and library on the second; bedroom, bath, and roof terrace on the third. A small home office fills a shed-like outbuilding in the garden. In order to emphasize the flow between the different spaces, the architects used expanded metal mesh on the steel stairs and railings and floor-to-ceiling glass at the rear of the house.

Although there is incredible light and visibility in the narrow townhouse, such an open design comes with challenges, especially when it comes to heating and cooling in the Swedish climate. Oscarson and Elding addressed these issues by careful selection of environmentally minded building technologies. Exterior walls are constructed of LECA sandwich blocks with integrated EPS insulation and the architects installed an air-source heat pump and a ventilation system that recycles return air as well as in-floor heating. A green sedum roof helps control day-to-night temperature fluctuations.

Blackbirds

Bestor Architecture
LOS ANGELES, CA
2015

Blackbirds, a multifamily housing development in Los Angeles's hilly Echo Park neighborhood is a creative example of how to thoughtfully navigate density on tight lots in urban areas. Designed by Barbara Bestor of L.A.–based firm Bestor Architecture for the developer LocalContract, the 18-unit project, like Buzz Court, follows Los Angeles's Small Lot Subdivision Ordinance. The design features four different type of two- and three-bedroom detached and semi-detached homes that, while not tiny, are modest single-family residences that range from around 1,400 to 1,900 square feet. The homes cluster around a Dutch *wooneft*, or living street, that is shared by cars, bikes, and pedestrians. This outdoor community space replaces the typical concrete driveway of traditional housing schemes.

As for the homes, Bestor took an approach that she calls "stealth density." Sensitive to the scale of the neighborhood, the rooflines mimic those of the surrounding single-family homes, full-grown trees are preserved on site, and the living street mitigates traffic impact. Inside, the house's functions are split between two or three floors: open kitchens and living areas, efficient bedrooms, and roof decks that overlook the hills of Echo Park.

"Blackbirds is a return to traditional housing in terms of how you fit into the landscape, but it is also a non-traditional developer model," Bestor explains, thinking about the texture of the urban fabric as formed by small-scale construction like in-law units rather than megablocks. "I have a romantic idea about individuals densifying L.A. as opposed to large developers doing twenty blocks at a time."

Buzz Court

Heyday Partnership
LOS ANGELES, CA
2013

Within the tiny house movement the emphasis is often simply on building an efficient home with the smallest possible square-footage. The contexts of these homes vary: sometimes they are on large rural plots of land, sometimes they are in a backyard or urban lot. The six single-family residences of Buzz Court designed by the Los Angeles design-build firm Heyday Partnership are not small, the two- and three-bedroom townhouses range from around 1,600 to 1,900 square feet. They do, however, present a compelling model for density-driven development in urban areas, often in response to the demand for much needed housing. A piece of urban infill, the project follows Los Angeles's Small Lot Subdivision Ordinance for subdivided lots, which permits townhouse-type development on lots that previously would not have not have met the size requirements of Los Angeles Municipal Code.The ordinance was created to help spur home construction and, although it has been controversial in some neighborhoods, thoughtful application of the legislation leads to innovative solutions.

Located on a busy street in the Silver Lake neighborhood, each of the six LEED-certified houses sits on its own parcel of land. Unlike some developments that create long and undistinguished driveways, Heyday Partnership's design is a twisting street. The homes alternate from side to side, which increases the sense of individual residences. The project's organization has the added benefit of reducing street noise across the site. A unique building screen made up of thin, white fins wraps all of Buzz Court—street-side, the fins act as a privacy screen, obscuring views into the living area, while allowing for light to penetrate and full views from the inside. By blocking direct solar gain, the fins also add to energy-saving calculations.

Each home follows the same basic model, although the floor plan adjusts for its location on the site: three stories with a garage taking up much of the ground floor and a roof deck with views of the Griffith Park Observatory. The second floor is dedicated to an open floor plan that links together the cooking, eating, and living areas. Bedrooms are compactly arranged on the third floor. Gone are the requisite front and back yards of suburbia—the generous rooftop decks change the paradigm of outdoor space. Although these homes are larger than what we would generally consider individual micro living, they present a vision of housing in a compact city.

Architects

Alma-nac Collaborative Architecture
—177
LONDON, UNITED KINGDOM
alma-nac.com

Alphaville Architects
—159
KYOTO, JAPAN
a-ville.net

Anonymous Architects
—171
LOS ANGELES, CA
anonymous-projects.com

Bestor Architecture
—195
LOS ANGELES, CA
bestorarchitecture.com

Bureau A
—13
GENEVA, SWITZERLAND
a-bureau.com

Centrala
—37
WARSAW, POLAND
centrala.net.pl

David Baker and Associates
—91
SAN FRANCISCO, CA
dbarchitect.com

EDGE Design Institute Ltd.
—85
HONG KONG, CHINA
edgedesign.com.hk

Elding Oscarson
—189
STOCKHOLM, SWEDEN
eldingoscarson.com

EZZO
—183
PORTO, PORTUGAL
ezzo.pt

Photography